People at Work
Making and Repairing Machines

Jan Champney   *Photographs by Chris Fairclough*

FRANKLIN WATTS
LONDON•SYDNEY

First published in 2008 by Franklin Watts
338 Euston Road, London NW1 3BH

Franklin Watts Australia
Level 17/207 Kent Street
Sydney NSW 2000

Editor: Julia Bird
Art Director: Jonathan Hair
Designer: Jane Hawkins
Photography: Chris Fairclough (unless otherwise credited)

Picture credits:
p.4: (bottom) Shutterstock © Lucian Coman; p.5: (top) Shutterstock © Christian Lagerek; p.8: Shutterstock © Arvind Balaraman; (bottom) Alamy © Ace Stock Limited/Alamy; p.9: Shutterstock © Ferenc Szelepcsenyi; p.16: Corbis © Kim Kulish/Corbis; p.17: (top) © istockphoto; (bottom) Shutterstock © Ingvar Tjostheim; p.20: (top) Shutterstock © mrfotos; (bottom) Shutterstock © Antonio Jorge Nunes; p.23: (bottom) istockphoto © Lise Gagne; p.24: istockphoto © Michael Krinke; p.25: (top) istockphoto © Michel de Nijs; (bottom) Shutterstock © Stephen McSweeny; p.26: Martyn Goddard, Goingreen, G-Wiz; p.27: (top) Shutterstock © Otmar Smit.

A CIP catalogue record for this book
is available from the British Library

ISBN: 978 0 7496 7820 3

Dewey Classification: 21.8

Printed in China

Franklin Watts is a division of Hachette Children's Books,
an Hachette Livre UK company.
www.hachettelivre.co.uk

Note to parents and teachers: Every effort has been made by the Publishers to ensure that the websites on p.31 of this book are suitable for children, that they are of the highest educational value, and that they contain no inappropriate or offensive material. However, because of the nature of the Internet, it is impossible to guarantee that the contents of these sites will not be altered. We strongly advise that Internet access is supervised by a responsible adult.

Contents

Machines and tools

Cranes are used to lift and move heavy materials.

The world is full of machines and equipment that help us at work, in our homes and other places.

Each machine or piece of equipment does a different task. On building sites and in factories and workshops there are special tools such as drills, cranes and **lathes** for drilling, lifting and shaping. Machines in hospitals help to save lives. Dishwashers and fridges help us in the home.

Ultrasound machines are used in hospitals to look inside patients' bodies.

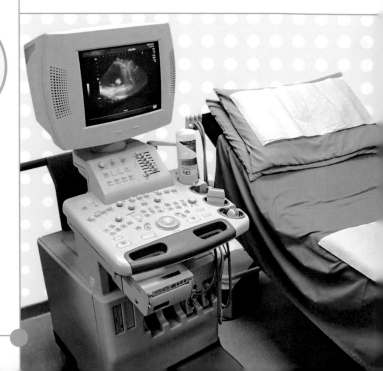

Key Questions

Think about your home.

What machines and tools do you have?

What materials are they made from?

What are they used for?

The people who build, repair, design and work with machines and tools are called **engineers**.

There are jobs for engineers in many different industries and sectors of work.

Engineers at work at an oil refinery.

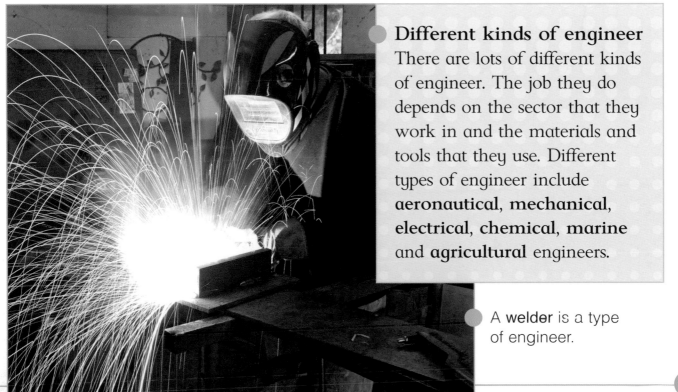

Different kinds of engineer
There are lots of different kinds of engineer. The job they do depends on the sector that they work in and the materials and tools that they use. Different types of engineer include **aeronautical**, **mechanical**, **electrical**, **chemical**, **marine** and **agricultural** engineers.

A **welder** is a type of engineer.

Craft, technician or professional?

There are three types of engineering job: **craft, technician** and **professional**.

Craft or mechanical engineers do more practical work than technician or professional engineers. There are lots of craft jobs. Some craft engineers work with or mend machines in factories and workshops. Others repair home appliances such as televisions and DVD players. Some work alone, others work in large teams.

Whatever they do, all craft engineers are trained to use different materials and equipment and must be able to follow technical instructions.

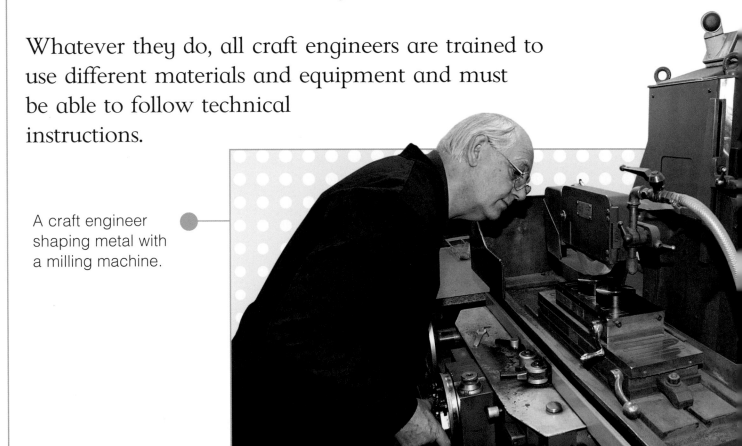

A craft engineer shaping metal with a milling machine.

A technician engineer repairing a machine that makes DVDs.

Technician engineers work in teams with craft and professional engineers. They design and develop new ideas and build, test and repair old and new machines. There are technician jobs in a variety of sectors of engineering.

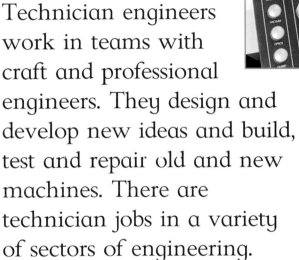

Key Questions

Why do you think craft, technician and professional engineers often work together in a team?

Qualifications

Most technician engineers need a special qualification such as a diploma to do their jobs. Most professional engineers require a degree in engineering from a college or university. This can be specialised in a particular area of engineering, such as IT or electrical engineering. Craft engineers often have qualifications such as NVQs (see p.31) but also learn a lot of their work on the job.

Professional engineers manage teams of craft and technician engineers. Although they must know how different equipment works, they usually do not do much practical work themselves.

Putting ideas onto paper

Every **product**, from a new car to an MP3 player, starts life on a drawing board.

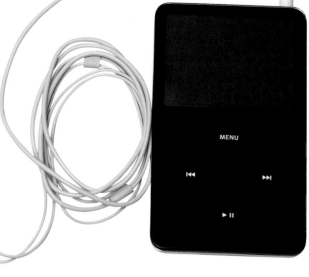

A draughtsperson using CAD to design a wheel fitting for a car.

Before craft engineers can begin building a machine, technician engineers called **draughtspeople** make drawings and instructions for them to follow.

Draughtspeople use a special program called Computer Aided Design (CAD) to create detailed 3D drawings that show what a machine should look like and how it will work. Draughtspeople also write instructions for the craft engineers to follow, so they need to understand engineering rules.

Giles is a draughtsperson in an aerospace company that makes engines for aeroplanes.

"My favourite subjects at school were design and technology, art, science and maths. When I left school I started an advanced **apprenticeship** to design parts for aeroplane engines. Sometimes these parts are very small and hidden away. Even though I can't always see them in action, it's good to know that my ideas do an important and useful job!"

Key Questions

What do you think are useful subjects to study if you want to be a draughtsperson?

What things do you think a draughtsperson has to consider when designing a machine such as a car or an MP3 player?

Every part of an aeroplane has been very carefully designed.

Working with metal

When a machine or product has been designed, the draughtperson's drawings and instructions are passed on to craft engineers.

John is a craft engineer in a factory that makes parts for cars.

John explains:
"I use tools and machinery to heat, bend and fold metal into the shapes on the drawings I am given. Lots of my work involves doing practical work using my hands, which can be tiring. I also do lots of measuring using special equipment. I try not to waste any metal as it's expensive, so there's a lot of maths in my job."

Metal workers use special machinery in the workshop.

A welder's job is joining or welding types of metal. Welders are craft engineers who work in lots of areas of mechanical engineering, including building cars and other vehicles, ship building and **construction**. They can work in big teams with other craft engineers or alone.

A welder sets to work using an arc welder.

Key Questions

What skills do you think metal workers need?

Why is it important for welders to follow health and safety rules?

Joining metal

Welding is a process that has been used for centuries. It usually involves heating two metal surfaces, then adding a molten material to stick them together. There are different types of welding, including arc, electric, gas and laser welding, and it can be done at sea, underwater and even in space!

Working with appliances

Some craft engineers repair and **maintain** domestic appliances such as washing machines, dishwashers and freezers. These engineers are known as **service and maintenance engineers.**

Paul helps to repair washing machines and tumble driers. He has set up his own mobile repair business, visiting people at home to mend their machines.

Paul says:
"I can normally repair a machine straight away, but sometimes I have to order a part and return to fit it. I used to work for a company that made washing machines. They paid me to do a college course. After I learned all about washing machine engines, I decided to start my own mobile repair service. I like being my own boss!"

Paul mends a faulty part on a tumble drier.

Other craft engineers repair office machinery such as printers and photocopiers. They visit offices and maintain or repair broken equipment, using special tools and cleaning chemicals.

Sam repairs photocopiers. He says: "I like my job as I get to spend a lot of time out and about. I use tools to carry out repair work on the photocopiers and do some electrical maintenance on them from time to time. I also clean the machines using special chemicals."

Key Questions

What skills do you think service and maintenance engineers need in their work?

Can you think of any other types of home or office equipment that require service and maintenance?

Working with motor vehicles

Some types of craft engineer work with cars and other motor vehicles. These engineers are known as motor vehicle technicians.

Some specialise in light vehicles, such as cars and motorbikes, while others work with heavier vehicles such as lorries. All motor vehicle technicians know how to check an engine for faults and will advise on the best way to repair them.

James (left) is a motor vehicle technician at a busy garage. "Working with cars is my dream job. After leaving school, I went to college where I did a BTEC course in vehicle repair and technology. I was lucky enough to get a job in a garage straight after leaving college and have worked there ever since. At first I just helped the other mechanics, but these days I have my own section and help to train new staff."

Other motor vehicle technicians specialise in working in particular areas of vehicle repair and maintenance.

Tyre and exhaust fitters replace or repair worn tyres and exhaust pipes. They have to learn to use different machines and special tools, such as jacks, spanners and wheel balancing machines.

Tom works as a tyre fitter.
"I work in a tyre-fitting garage. I meet lots of people during the day. I have to look up the size and type of tyre that they need and give advice. Worn tyres are very dangerous so I'm proud that my work helps to keep people safe in their cars."

Tom prepares to change a tyre using a floor jack.

Specialist mechanics
Other motor vehicle technician jobs specialising in certain areas include:
- vehicle body and paintwork
- vehicle electrics
- roadside recovery and assistance.

At sea

Not all engineering jobs take place on dry land. Marine engineers work out at sea, as well as in shipyards.

Marine engineers spend most of their time working in the ship's engine room.

Engine room
The ship's machinery is kept in the engine room. Conditions can be hot, noisy and dangerous due to the fuel stored in the room, so engineers have to follow strict safety rules.

Marine engineers help to design, build and repair ships, boats, tankers and even submarines! The tools they use depend on the type of ship or boat and what materials it is made of. These materials include metal, **fibre glass**, plastic and wood. As well as maintaining the engine and outside of a ship, marine engineers work on the areas used by the crew. Some marine engineers spend weeks on a ship at a time.

Some marine engineers work on **oil rigs** or platforms that are stationed far out at sea.

Martin is a drilling engineer on an oil rig. "My job is to make sure that drilling takes place safely and effectively, and with as little damage to the sea environment as possible. The rig is anchored far out at sea, so I travel there by helicopter. I stay on the rig for two weeks at a time. It can be windy, wet and cold, but we have recreation rooms and a gym and all our food is provided."

Oil rig workers wear bright, protective clothing.

Safety

Oil and gas rigs can be hazardous places. Weather conditions and wind strength can be extreme far out at sea, and rigs are always at risk from fire because of the explosive nature of the fuels that workers drill for. Rig workers wear protective clothing at all times and are air-lifted off the rig immediately if there is any hint of a fire. Most workers also spend two weeks away from a rig for every two weeks spent on it, so that they can rest, relax and spend time with their families.

This oil rig is stationed in the North Sea.

Research and testing

Research is an important part of the job for **engineering technicians.**

Roger works for a company that helps to design new cars. His job is to test out the different engine parts before they are put in place.

Roger says:
"When each new part is designed, I carry out lots of tests to make sure it is safe. I have to check if the part will work properly under different conditions and I sometimes use specialised computer programs to help me find this out. I studied engineering technology at college for three years before qualifying as an engineering technician. My job is important because we have to be sure that people will be safe in our cars."

Engineering technicians like Roger help to keep cars on the road.

Some engineering machines have to measure and cut very small lengths and widths of metal to use in machines and engines. It is very important that the machines used to measure these lengths of metal work properly.

Chris is using an instrument called a vernier scale to take a measurement.

Measurement and control technicians like Chris check the machines regularly.

Chris explains:
"I use particular tools to check the machine is accurate. If a part is even just millimetres too long or too wide, the engine or part won't work properly and can be damaged. This costs lots of money to put right and can be dangerous."

Key Questions

What skills do you think engineering technicians need in their work?

Technicians often work in teams. What makes someone a good teamworker?

Electrical and telecommunications

Electrical and telecommunications engineers build and maintain the systems that carry electrical and telecommunication signals.

Electricity cables supply homes and businesses with power.

Ali says:

"I work in a team with people from the construction sector. My job is to plan where the electricity cables and wires should go before construction can begin on new buildings and roads. People's safety is our top priority, so it's important that we work together as a team. Working with electricity can be dangerous, so we look after our equipment and tools very carefully and wear protective clothing."

Key Questions

What protective clothing do electrical engineers wear?

Why do you think they wear it?

Every day people use telephones, the Internet and satellite television. Telecommunications engineers lay, maintain and repair the huge **cable**, **fibre optic** and satellite networks that transport these signals around the world.

Paul is a telecommunications technician for a telephone company.

Paul says:
"I help to repair faults in the telephone network in my area. Customers ring a hotline to report any problems and I travel to their homes or businesses in my van with all my tools. If I can mend it there and then I will, otherwise I bring it back to our workshop for more work. I spend a lot of time on the road but I like the variety in my job."

Telecommunications technicians use specialised tools to detect faults in telephone networks.

Chemical engineers

Chemical engineers are responsible for turning **raw materials** into new, useful products.

Chemical engineers, also known as process engineers, work in a variety of sectors, such as energy supply, food and drink production and the medicine industry. They help to work out the best way to turn a material into a product that people can use.

A chemical engineer using a machine called a micrometer to test some plastic.

Saskia is a chemical engineer. She says:
"I work in a company that makes plastic products. I look after the equipment and machines that make the plastic. I work with different machinery and use special chemicals in my work. I have to consider whether the way we're making the plastic is the safest, most cost-effective and environmentally friendly way possible, so there's always a lot to think about!"

A chemical engineer at work in a plastic processing plant.

Some chemical engineers help to design the processes that make products, while others help to design the machinery that makes the products or the plants where they are made.

Chemical engineers help to make cosmetics, among many other things.

Health and safety
Chemical engineers have to follow strict health and safety rules as this can be dangerous work. They wear goggles and often have to put on protective clothing. Accidents can easily happen if people do not take care as they work.

Agricultural engineers

Agricultural engineers design and repair the different machines used in farming and crop production. These machines include milking machines, tractors and ploughing and cutting equipment.

Susie is an agricultural engineer.
"I always knew I wanted a career that combined farming and engineering. My family are farmers, but I always enjoyed driving and repairing the tractors more than looking after the animals. When I finished school, I took agricultural engineering at college. I now have a job in a company that makes tractors and ploughing equipment. We design new products, test them out and then sell them around the world."

A combine harvester separates wheat from the husks to make grain and straw.

John is also an agricultural engineer, but his job involves very different work.

John says:
"My job involves biology, physics and engineering. I help farmers and growers to grow better crops by laying **irrigation** systems and pipes on their land. We use similar equipment to the machines used in the construction sector. Irrigation helps water to drain away when it's raining, but lets the ground be watered when it's dry. I love working outdoors and am happy knowing that my job is helping farmers."

John inspects an irrigation system that he has set up in a tulip field.

Key Questions

What other jobs involve growing or looking after plants?

What subjects do you think would be useful for this job?

A farm irrigation system in action, watering a potato field.

Working with energy

Energy engineers work to keep our homes and businesses supplied with heat and electricity.

Some energy engineers help to find the **fossil fuels** of oil, coal and natural gas. They work in mines, off shore and on land. They work in teams with scientists and **geologists**. Many work overseas.

Other engineers work towards reducing the effects of **climate change**. They are helping to design new machines that use less fossil fuel, or changing existing machines to become more **energy efficient**.

The G-Wiz car was designed by energy engineers. It runs on an electric battery.

Sean is an oil engineer. He describes how engineers find suitable sites using rock samples (see above). "Finding sites for oil can be hard work. We use special drilling machinery and laboratory equipment to sample the rock. When we find oil or gas we work out how far down to drill and which tools to use."

Roof solar panels are a good way of turning sunlight into energy. Energy engineers are working to find ways of making them more affordable.

Others types of engineers, known as **environmental engineers**, look for new forms of energy. They work in teams with scientists to find new ways of making energy by using the power of water, wind or the Sun.

Renewable energy

Energy sources that will not run out, such as wind, water and sunlight, are known as **renewable energy**. As the world's fossil fuels are now close to running out, renewable energy is seen as one of the ways forward. The European Union is aiming to make renewable sources produce 20 per cent of our energy by 2020.

This wind farm off the coast of Norfolk produces enough power to supply more than 40,000 homes.

The finishing touches

When the different engineers have done their work, other add the finishing touches.

Paint sprayers wear protective clothing, such as overalls and masks.

Paint sprayers are craft engineers who use special painting equipment. They paint car panels, large machines and engines, and even parts of planes! As well as making a machine look more attractive, painting also helps to protect it from the weather.

Tom is a panel sprayer. "I work in a garage painting car panels. I also make minor repairs to bodywork. I wasn't sure what I wanted to do when I left school but I knew I wanted to work with cars and motorbikes. I did some work experience in a local garage, trying out various jobs and found I enjoyed the panel spraying most, so I looked for a job as a panel sprayer."

Quality controllers work in every area of engineering. They can work at a technician or professional level. Their job is to make sure each finished product or machine is safe. They use special equipment, such as x-ray and ultrasound machines, to show up any mistakes.

A quality controller using a voltmeter to check a piece of machinery.

Andrew is a quality controller for an electronics company.
"I check everything to make sure it is safe, strong and won't break down. If I find something isn't right I either reject it or send it back for more work. I have to be very strict with the rules - that's my job!"

? Key Questions

Can you think of any other jobs you could try out if you were doing work experience at a garage?

What skills does a quality controller need to have?

Glossary

Aeronautical engineer An engineer who works on designing, making and maintaining parts for aircraft.

Agricultural engineer An engineer who designs and makes farming machinery.

Apprenticeship A work placement where a young person can learn a trade.

Cable A thick bundle of wires that carry electrical or telecommunications signals.

Chemical engineer An engineer who works on the processes that turn raw materials into products such as food and drink and medicines.

Climate change A gradual change in the world's weather patterns.

Construction Making and repairing buildings and structures.

Craft engineer An engineer who does mainly practical work. Also known as a mechanical engineer.

Draughtsperson Someone who makes very detailed drawings of machines or buildings.

Electrical engineer An engineer who works with electricity supply.

Energy efficient A product that is designed to save energy.

Engineer Someone who designs, makes or repairs machines.

Engineering technician A technician who uses engineering principles in their work.

Environmental engineer An engineer who is involved in looking for new sources of energy.

Fibre glass A type of glass. It is light and very strong.

Fibre optics Glass or plastic threads that carry light signals. They are widely used in telecommunications.

Fossil fuels Oil, coal and natural gas.

Geologist A scientist who works with soil and rocks.

Irrigation Supplying land with water.

Lathe Engineering tool that shapes metal.

Maintain To keep in a state of good repair.

Marine engineer An engineer who works on a ship or oil rig, or in a shipyard.

Mechanical engineer *See craft engineer.*

Oil rig An oil drilling station, often located off shore.

Product Something that is made.

Professional engineer An engineer who manages teams of craft and technical engineers.

Quality controller Someone who makes sure products are up to the required standard.

Raw materials Natural products, such as wood, water and metals.

Renewable energy Energy from a source that will not run out, such as the Sun, wind or water.

Research To find out as much as possible about a topic, event or person.

Service and maintenance engineers Engineers who look after and repair home and office appliances.

Technician engineer An engineer who works with craft and professional engineers to design and develop new ideas and build, test and repair old and new machines.

Welder A craft engineer who welds or joins metal surfaces.

Skills and Training

You now know that the engineering sector has lots of different jobs on offer.

Many need special skills and training. You can get these skills by going to college or university. However, there are some jobs that can be done with only a small amount of training.

Training and qualifications table

Aeronautical engineer Agricultural engineer Chemical engineer Electrical engineer Energy engineer Environmental engineer Quality controller Telecommunications engineer	Degree or higher level qualification
Draughtsperson Motor vehicle technician Engineering research technician Marine engineer technician Telecommunications technician Quality controller	2-3 A levels BTEC National Level 3 diploma NVQ level 3
Welder Service and maintenance engineer Auto electrician Roadside recovery and assistance Vehicle body repairer Paint sprayer	4-5 GCSEs including Maths and Science Level 2 Diploma NVQ level 2
Tyre and exhaust fitter	GCSEs grades D-F Level 1 Diploma NVQ level 1 Good practical skills

The table above shows the normal minimum qualifications needed for each job. There will be times when more or fewer qualifications are needed, so use the table only as a guide!

The qualifications you can take depend on what is on offer in your area. Ask your careers teacher or Connexions PA for advice.

Further information

For more information on engineering, contact the following organisations:

British Marine Industry
Tel: 01784 473377
www.britishmarine.co.uk

Cogent
Tel: 01925 515200
www.cogent-ssc.com

Engineering Careers Information Service
Tel: 0800 282167
www.enginuity.org.uk

Engineering Council UK
Tel: 020 3206 0500
www.engc.org.uk

Institution of Agricultural Engineers
Tel: 01525 861096
www.iagre.org.uk

Institution of Chemical Engineers
Tel: 01788 578214
www.whynotchemeng.com

Institution of Engineering and Technology
Tel: 01438 313311
www.theiet.org

Institution of Mechanical Engineers
Tel: 020 7222 7899
www.imeche.org.uk

Oilcareers
Tel: 0870 870 4564
www.oilcareers.com

SEMTA
Tel: 01923 238441
www.semta.org.uk

Index